Acknowledgements

Sincere thanks to all two- and four-legged friends who have supported me in the creation of this book: the Thomas Kren family with moggies Nicky and Lisa; the Lausecker family and their cats; Christine and Dominik Rappaport with their sixteen little paws; Carmen Windhaber with Willow and Paola; Sarah Nettel with Bibi and Benco, as well as Renate Trost and her kittens. A big thanks to our photographer, Kurt Kracher, who sacrificed many hours of relaxation and was always there at just the right moment!

I would also like to thank my beloved partner, Wolfgang, for his assistance, his optimism, his inspiration, and much more. A loving thanks also to my mother for her support. Thanks to my 17-year old female cat, Coco, who has accompanied me during the writing of all my books. A grateful thankyou paw print for our mixed breed dog, Snowy, for her patience when her walks were sometimes cut short if I was in the middle of a chapter.

My editor, Alice Rieger, thoroughly deserves a mention for her excellent work and her patience during the writing of this book.

The author would like to thank the Trixie company very much for the generous provision of equipment and accessories shown in the photographs. All items shown are available from the Trixie company (www.trixie.de).

Contents

captivating games

Play is not just a great way to pass the time, it also improves communication and social contact, increases physical fitness, regulates emotions, and gives an animal the motivation to learn. Play offers both animal and human a wealth of possibilities that are too good to be ignored!

Playing – a serious business

Playing is just a bit of fun, isn't it? Actually, play is essential for both adolescent and adult creatures, allowing an animal to learn by experience without serious consequences. It's not just dolphins, whales, primates, and rodents who have a life-long interest in play, so, too, do our domestic cats. Our four-legged friends are curious and open-minded about their environment and the challenges it represents – not just when they are kittens, but as adults, too. They put their heart and soul into play, whether alone or together with their feline friends. However, their preferred playing partner is usually their owner.

What could be more fun than playing with your siblings and exploring your environment?

Hiding, exploring, and observation are all skills which are learnt during play.

All that play is exhausting; even kittens need a rest every now and again.

Fit for life

Kitten play is energetic, and fascinating to watch. They scamper through the house, follow each other over chairs and beds, side-step and swerve as quickly as rabbits, and rear up and pounce in an attempt to overthrow their opponent. Their playful behaviour is often quite over the top, in contrast to how they would behave in a serious situation. During play, kittens move with exaggerated effort, greater speed, and more frequently repeat actions. Willingness to play is expressed by facial gestures and body language, so that a playful attack is not mistaken for an aggressive attack, and doesn't lead to serious confrontation.

Playtime should occur in a relaxed atmosphere and be spontaneous. Only if a cat is in a familiar environment and feels at ease can he enjoy play. Animals that are stressed, anxious or ill won't be as playful, or will stop playing altogether.

Rough and tumble

Small kitten siblings love to play-fight, and run around with boundless energy. Different instinctive behaviours, such as hunting, are shown during play which improve a kitten's perception and responsiveness. During play, kittens store useful experiences in their memory and test out new solutions, thus improving their performance and fitness. Also, brain cells form new neural pathways (neural tracts connecting one part of the nervous system with another) so that the learning ability of the animal is constantly improving. The cat will playfully try out all the things he has learnt on his owners as well, so beware! Play is significant, not only for the development of kittens during the growth phase, but at every age. The neural pathways of animals who learn all the time and live in an exciting environment have more branches than those of animals who do not get an opportunity to play. Playful animals are usually thought of as being bright, curious, and intellectually active.

Get a head start ...

Siblings begin playing together from the fourth week of life, and tail off around the twelfth

The mother cat is a good teacher. Hunting lessons, good manners, and cleanliness are all required subjects for kittens, and mum monitors each learning step very carefully.

to fourteenth week. In the first scuffles, teeth are tried and tested. A popular game object is mum, and she is usually very patient if her offspring mistake her for a climbing frame, or bite her tail.

At about six weeks, co-ordination of movement is so pronounced that the little devils can give wild chases, alternate between attack and defence, and try out their pouncing skills. These social games improve confidence and encourage the kittens to use trial and error. The kitten will experience rebuffs from the other players, or the mother cat, if he bites too hard or misuses his claws! From about the seventh and eighth week, kittens begin to play with objects. This is the period where a cat's movements become more visually co-ordinated, and they can catch small, moving objects. They will play with anything that falls

into their paws and arouses their interest: Does it move, rustle or squeak? Or perhaps it has an interesting smell?

Social skills

Play is important for social development; our companion animals learn how to build relationships and strengthen bonds with one another. They gain experience in dealing with other types of animals, and quickly learn how to control their own aggression. A kitten will soon learn what happens when he bites too hard: his playmate turns away, bats him with a paw, or even bites back! And he'll also try it on with us, too! Intensive play – and thus positive experiences with his people – will make our cat an open-minded and contented companion, and for us bi-peds, playing is a great way to gain the trust and affection of our

During play, a cat will bare her teeth if her playmate has gone too far. This is the only way the kitten will learn how far he can go and when to stop.

Her playmate's toy is far more interesting than her own!

Fun and games for cats!

four-legged friend, and enhance the human-animal relationship. Significantly, cats whose owners play with them every day are reported to have fewer behavioural problems.

Strategic play

Adult animals use play as a strategy to solve conflict and release pent-up stress. The roles of attacker and defender alternate, so that no one is a winner or loser. The game also serves as a ploy to divert attention away from any serious intentions.

During play between humans and animals, the game will also be used to test limits. Your four-legged friend is seeing how far he can bend the rules so he can put this new knowledge to everyday use with you. It was Albert Einstein who said: "Play is the highest form of research."

Pussycat training

Hiding, creeping, jumping, catching prey – these are the favourite pastimes of a born hunter and therefore the basis of all feline games. Animals in the wild are confronted by the challenges of their environment on a daily basis; they have to adapt to constantly changing situations, and call on past experiences in an instant. Since this kind of training is not possible for an indoor cat, daily play with his owner is very important. The perfect cat toy should appeal to those senses used for hunting, such as sight, hearing, and touch. Cats prefer moving toys or those that come to life when moved about by their owner.

Playing is hunting

It's not just cats that are allowed outside who love hunting; our indoor cats will transform from cuddly puss to predator in seconds, given half the chance. Cats are hunters who use cover as concealment as they approach their prey, and then attack at close range. Acoustic signals, such as scratching, rustling

With an expert swipe, Willow attempts to snare the 'mouse.'

Capturing prey requires complete focus and precision.

Kit bits
WHAT PURPOSE DOES PLAY FULFIL?

- Hones physical skills

- Trains perception and reaction time

- Increases repertoire of behaviour

- Helps dispel aggression and learning to control own aggression (control of bite intensity and learning the bite inhibition)

- Aids the formation and maintenance of social organisations and structures (socialisation process)

- Promotes a stable social order and development of social roles

- Can be used by adult animals as a strategy to resolve conflict

- Improves knowledge of the environment

- Relieves boredom

- Releases pent-up energy

- Reinforces boundaries

- Deepens bonds between peers, and strengthens the human-animal relationship

the house, so a game using hunting skills is the best way to maintain physical and mental fitness, and use up any excess energy. It's also a great opportunity for you to join in and play games with your cat.

Hunting skills
At the age of just five weeks, the playful kittens begin to hone their actions to ensure they will one day be first-class hunters. Many different types of hunting skills are displayed during play. Mouse-catching, fishing (or hooking things with the paws), and bird watching behaviour are all evident when a cat plays with toys such as a stuffed mouse, or ping-pong balls, for example.

Kit bits
HUNTING WITHOUT HUNGER

Cats will hunt even if they are not hungry, and there is no evidence to suggest that a hungry cat catches mice more skilfully than an animal who is well-fed. Even cats that are fed very well by their owners will still be motivated by the visual and auditory stimuli of prey.

However, as stalking and catching prey requires a lot of energy, it is likely that animals who are weakened by hunger will not be as successful during the hunt as an animal that is in top form.

or squeaky sounds, will encourage most cats to search for prey. Predatory behaviour is usually instigated by a moving object.

Cats who play outside enjoy up to six hours a day of hunting, whilst indoor cats play for less than one hour a day. Some domestic tigers have to act out their hunting instinct in

Fun and games for cats!

Paola watches intently as her owner skilfully moves a mouse. She is ready to attack: the mouse has her full attention and she is about to pounce.

Mouse-catcher

The cat sits perfectly still, hind legs tensed. The upper body straightens, he will appear to wiggle side-to-side and, with outstretched paws, pounces on his prey. It is interesting to note that the cat doesn't jump up to catch his prey, but prefers to pounce on it from above.

Fishing

To pull a fish out of the water and onto land requires not only patience and perseverance, but also a lot of skill and strength. The experienced hunter lurks patiently on the bank until a fish appears at the surface. With

extended claws and a targeted strike of the paw, the prey is hooked and thrown onto land, in a similar action to that of bears during the annual salmon hunt.

The high jump

If you use a toy mouse when playing with your cat, you'll know this move.

The cat tries to reach the prey with an outstretched paw and extended claws. If he can't quite reach the object of desire, he sits up and tries to catch it with both paws, then follows this with a jump from a standstill high into the air.

Game tips

Breaks

Respect your cat's peace and quiet. If your cat is asleep, don't wake him up for a game. After feeding time, playing and jumping around are a bad idea, because the digestive system needs time to do its work

Come and play with me!

Choice

Find specific playful activities which suit the needs and preferences of your cat. A cat who can play outside and satisfy his hunting instinct will not be quite so enamoured with indoor games. Kittens play differently to older animals, who may already be showing signs of health problems. Cats who don't have any other feline playmates tend to show a stronger desire to play with people

Duration

Play with your cat every day. The recommended time for playing with your indoor cat is about an hour, divided into three to five sessions, according to the natural activity rhythm of your cat. If the game doesn't seem to appeal then shorten it, or if your cat seems to be enjoying himself play for a little while longer

The nodules on the hedgehog balls make this toy unpredictable, stimulating the prey instinct. The ball jumps one way, then suddenly bounces in the opposite direction.

Effect

Play helps dispel pent-up energy and stress, so your cat will therefore be more relaxed and happier if you play with him. Daily interaction with your puss also strengthens your relationship with him

End the game

You decide when to play and when to stop, making playtime a highlight of the day for your domestic tiger. After some fun-filled interaction between you, clear away the toys until the next game session. Toys which are permanently available lose their appeal

Environment

The type of game and playing time should be adjusted according to climatic conditions and the local environment. Some animals are sensitive to heat. And be watchful for any risk of injury to human or animal within the household

Limits

Note physical and mental limits and differences between individuals, such as age, breed, nature, individual maturity, health, and experience. Young animals can't focus on a particular game as long as older felines, and, even with adult animals, their physical condition and ability to concentrate should be taken into account. Breaks safeguard the animal against physical and emotional fatigue

Fun and games for cats!

Motivation
Toys should be motivational objects. The choice of toy affects the game's success. After playing learning and intelligence games, celebrate the success of an exercise with a reward for your cat, such as petting or a treat. If he doesn't get the task right, on no account tell him off – this is an absolute no-no!

Partners
Make the time to play a game with your cat. They may seem to have a great time with their own kind, but plenty of attention from you is still their favourite thing!

Play types
Every cat owner knows that his cat is a creature with unique characteristics, and individual strengths and weaknesses, which means that each animal has his own preference for what games to play (see the game-type test on page 18

Prey
Choose toys which are the same size as a cat's real prey. The feline prey spectrum includes rodents such as burrowing or field mice, small reptiles, and small birds and insects. Toys that are much larger than potential prey animals are often ignored

Ritual
Daily fixed times for games and cuddles reassure him and strengthen your bond

Success
Play should be fun and pleasurable. End the game on a high note, such as letting him catch and play with the toy mouse or ball

Taboo
Never offer your hands or fingers to play-fight or hunt in any game as you could be injured!

After the game, a break in play is in order. Indoor cats spend up to eighteen hours a day sleeping.

Bibi enjoys attention from her owner. If she has had enough of being cuddled, she shows this clearly through her facial expressions and body language. This is the time to leave her be and look forward to the next cuddle.

Tempo
Take rest breaks as younger animals can't focus for too long on one thing. Over-enthusiastic games or boisterous team-mates can cause stress and strain, especially in kittens who may be a little anxious. Let games end quietly, so that your puss can calm down and relax

Times
Cats love routine and always do certain things at set times. Just like free-roaming cats, our house cats are most active in the dusk and

evening hours, which is the best time to try a game with your cat

Toys
Ideally, toys should satisfy all of the senses: eyes, nose, ears, paws, and claws! When looking for a cat toy, make sure it's safe and suitable for play purposes

Willingness
Finish the game before your feline friend loses interest. Cats show quite clearly whether or not they are interested in a game

What kind of game to play?

A Detective and sniffer pro

Everything and everyone in the house has to be investigated and sniffed thoroughly, including his owner's pockets. The special skills of his super-nose should be put to use by tracking down treats

Give your cat a Snack Ball, or invent small tasks where food is offered as a reward. Scent games, for example, involving a catnip pouch, are a great idea

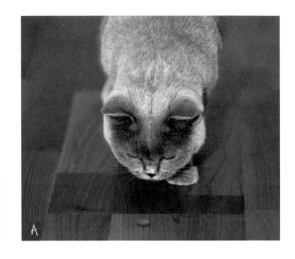

A

B

B Brawler and fighter

He may scuffle with other cats, but also loves playing with cushions or toys. Everything gets chased, especially his owner's feet – a particular attraction

Use a mix of thinking and fun games with movement to get the perfect balance. Chase him through the house, make him a climbing rope, or get him to do some cat-tree gymnastics to use up some of that excess energy

C Acrobat and athlete

No shelf is too high and no ball rolls too far. Climbing and running are a passion, and he has boundless energy

Hunting games are considered great fun by this cat, especially when playing ball games that demand speed and accuracy. He tends to play nicely with people and with other cats. Also a huge fishing fan, given half the chance!

C

D The entertainer

Inventive, loves toys, and even the slightest whiff of boredom will have him turning the house upside down

Sufficient physical and mental exercise is required, and running, romping, and climbing are his favourite types of fun. Also, objects that are hiding in boxes are one of the highlights of his day. He particularly enjoys a game with his owner

E Softie

This cat is often quite nervous of new toys, and it takes some time before he begins to show confidence

Gentle games with his people and cuddles bring him great comfort. Less confident animals should play games they find easy, in order to build their self-confidence. He also enjoys hiding games, where he can see everyone and everything, but nobody can see him!

F Games critique

Ordinary toys are too boring: toys must rattle or squeak

When his owner plays along and the objects come to life, this will motivate the games-meister! Anything with feathers on is high on the hit list because this stimulates his hunting instinct. But the Snack Ball is also very appealing if, every now and then, a delicious reward falls out

Home alone cat

As long as hunting instincts and senses are stimulated by the right games, cats also enjoy playing alone. Depending on the temperament of the animal, he may like a laid-back activity or a crazy runabout. Your puss not only enjoys physical activity, he also loves to put his thinking cap on

Solo games for loners

When he pushes the cube with his paw, it starts to flash. Now kitty must decide whether to pursue the flickering light, or ignore the object and walk away!

Play holds boredom at bay, creates adventures, and keeps an animal physically and mentally fit. This is especially essential for indoor cats, who may be on their own during the day without companions for company.

They require a balanced activity programme to keep them occupied which should meet the requirements of our naturally-predatory cats. Your cat is a born hunter who likes exploring, hiding, stalking, and catching prey – all of which set the benchmark for a successful game. The game and the toy should appeal to those senses used during the hunt. If a toy requires that your cat use his eyes, ears, and paws, it's like to satisfy even the most demanding moggy.

Bring on the toys!

Cats are happy to play alone, especially if the toy is appealing. While humans expect their toys to be of good quality and colourful design, cats have other requirements, such as being able to move it around with their paws. Some cats have favourite toys right from when they were a kitten, whilst others are always on the lookout for new stimulation. Besides furry toy mice and ping-pong balls, small objects from everyday human life are often chosen as favourite toys. Every cat owner can think of something of theirs which has been turned into a cat toy.

Variety

Balls, whatever the variations on the classic, inspire the majority of cats. A light pat with the paw or a little push from human hands, and the ball begins to roll enticingly across the floor. Balls come in many styles and in various materials such as rubber, leather, fabric, plush, or plastic. Most pet shops sell balls, from a simple ball through to a luxury toy that glows in the dark, rolls by itself, or makes a rustling noise when it moves.

Kit bits
BALLS

Category:	Physical games
Suitable for:	Cats of all ages
Effect:	Improves co-ordination, physical and mental fitness; helps use excess energy
Important:	Balls should be a certain size so that they cannot be accidentally swallowed by the cat when playing. Marbles are unsuitable for play, and larger-sized balls are not so easy for little cat paws to handle

Fun and games for cats!

Run for it

Balls are ideal because they awaken the hunting instinct, and encourage your cat to chase his fleeing prey. Especially popular are table tennis balls or similar lightweight balls, which are available specifically for cats in pet shops. They disappear under shelves and beds, and rebound off the walls. Try dropping several ping-pong balls from a metre or so away, and let kitty choose which he will chase. He may be so excited by the numerous balls that he can't decide which one to go after!

These balls are great fun and ideal for an active puss. They are safe, cheap, and you can never have enough of them.

Disco fever

In addition to the usual, balls also come in the shape of hedgehogs or cubes. When movement or vibration is sensed, these flash in two colours, making the toys unpredicatable and therefore interesting. Hedgehog balls are great fun because, when you throw them, they bounce in different, unexpected directions. The sudden change in direction, and being able to move the ball with their paws, makes the toy very exciting for most cats.

A quick bat of the paw sends the ball flying and the game begins again.

Snack balls

Especially popular are so-called snack balls or activity balls made of plastic that are filled with dry food. As your cat pushes the ball along the floor, a morsel of dry food will eventually drop out through a small opening, encouraging him to keep playing with the ball. This activity satisfies the hunting instinct, and can help prevent boredom and stress.

A positive side effect is that kitty has to work for his food, meaning he will expend more energy and keep weight gain in check. But be careful to ensure you deduct the dry food in the snack ball from the daily food ration.

After a wild chase through the house, Benco believes he has the ball firmly under control ...

... so it's a bit of a shock for the hunter when the supposedly dead 'prey' suddenly bounces back!

Some cats develop into professional ball players, and can get a snack out straight away – they quickly learn which direction the ball needs to be pushed for the food to drop out.

These balls are perfect for occupying bored house cats, and are a great way to encourage your cat to hunt for his food. Also, because cats naturally prefer small snacks to large meals, it is an ideal way to feed your pet. If given his daily food ration all at once, your cat will naturally tend to eat this in ten to 16 servings during the day.

Roll on playtime
Cats are inventive in their choice of toy: a ball of paper patted from the desk, a wine cork from the coffee table, a piece of uncooked pasta, or even a stolen olive from the kitchen are fair game. If the item can be easily moved and smells interesting, it will be irresistible to cats. Everyday items are an inexpensive alternative to traditional cat toys, and also offer plenty of variety. Most cats like to play with bottle caps, bits of plastic, buttons, or straws. Even the trusty old wooden top, which you might remember from your childhood, can amuse a cat for hours. However, allowing your cat to play with rubber bands, sharp objects or small parts that can be swallowed is not a good idea. Be aware of which everyday objects your cat likes to play with, and check that they are safe, in terms of shape and material.

Toy mice

Most cats would agree that you can never have enough mice. Furry or squeaky mice in various sizes, with or without a catnip scent, can be patted around, and provide hours of fun. To keep the game interesting, have just one or two mice available at a time. Clear away the remaining mice and offer your cat a different mouse each time.

Furry toy mice are high on the list of the most popular cat toys. The fur feels similar to real mouse fur in his mouth, and the toy can be easily patted about the house. When you choose a toy mouse, be mindful of size. In the wild, larger rodents and rats are regarded as opponents, and usually given a wide berth.

Toy mice bigger than the size of a large rodent are therefore not as popular with cats.

Feathers

In addition to chasing balls or toy mice, cats also enjoy playing with feathers. How about a feather tied to a piece of string? It's very light, and the cat can pat it into the air and chase it. There are many toys with feathers that 'bounce back,' and so are ideal for solitary games. After each blow of the paw, the feather flies back and is ready for the next attack.

For cats, hunting a feather toy is almost as exciting as hunting a real bird. All you need is a light touch to move the feather and arouse the interest of your little predator. A featherlight

Naughty Nicky has stolen olives from the kitchen to play with.

Fun and games for cats!

What's the state of play with this mouse; it's not moving ...

... maybe I can breathe life into it?

Not many cats enjoy hunting super-sized mice: Bibi has two!

Kit bits
TOY MICE

Category:	Toys for retrieving, hunting, and prey games with a 'license to kill'
Suitable for:	Cats of all ages
Benefits:	Sharpens hunting skills, improves physical and mental fitness, and helps use up excess energy
Important:	Do not let your cat play with very small mice that have detachable eyes or parts that are easy to swallow

toy is well suited to solitaire games and can be carried around in a cat's mouth. Since cats may chew on feathers, there's a risk of injury from their sharp ends, so please ensure you supervise your cat when he is playing with these. After the game, the feather toys should be stowed away, ready for next time.

Fishing fun for skilful paws
Cats are avid hunters and frequently demonstrate perseverance and skill in order to catch potential prey. Cats who are allowed outside will hunt for up to six hours at a time, although is usually successful only one in every 15 attempts.

Experienced hunters are used to investing time in catching their prey, and can't allow themselves to be discouraged by failure.

Invisible prey
Games where the toy must first be found and then caught before it can be played with are particularly exciting, as they elicit curiosity, which gets the cat involved as he tries to locate the prize. Many pet shops sell different toys for tactile games such as this, like the well-known colourful plush cube that has a cross-cut opening on all four sides, and on the top. Inside the cube are four fluffy balls. The cat has to insert his paw inside the cube and retrieve the balls before being able to play with them.

This toy is usually popular with most cats, but the plush cube is a bit soft and not very stable, and tends to collapse in on itself when played with, which could mean that you cat will lose interest relatively quickly.

This toy made of straw and feathers is very appealing to felines. Featherlight, it can be dashed back and forth between the paws, caught in the air, and pounced on.

Try filling the cube with different toys to keep it exciting. A shoe box with a lid and two to three holes cut in the side will fulfil the same purpose, and be a little more stable for enthusiastic patting games.

The toys inside the box should be made out of a material that is easy to grip with the claws or paws, such as leather or sisal (a kind of carpet-like material).

The 'Swiss cheese' toy

This cube toy looks like a piece of Swiss cheese. On the surface and the sides are openings through which balls with bells on

The mouse goes round and round, just waiting to be caught by an attentive predator.

At last he has it in his paws!

The mouse has been rubbed with the intoxicating smell of catnip.

Play is not only fun, but also essential for the development of young cats, and important for the human-animal relationship, because trust is established when playing together.

The 'Swiss cheese' comes complete with a small play rod and three balls to provide great entertainment. The cat can feel for the ball with his paws, or hunt the mouse on the rod.

can be moved inside the object. Put some pieces of dried food or other small toys in the Swiss cheese so that your cat can hook them out – an ideal activity for a cat who has to occupy himself during the day.

Since it is almost – but not totally – impossible for the cat to fish out the balls from the 'Swiss cheese,' he may become frustrated. Watch your cat as he plays. If his interest declines sharply and he shows signs of displeasure, end the game on a positive note by hiding a treat or a morsel of dried food in one of the holes. This way, Killy will find the food, associate this treat with the game, and will be more likely to show interest next time around.

Many pet shops sell toys such as Cat Turbo Tracks, which looks a little like a mini roller-coaster for balls. The balls rattle and run down various tubes, which the cat finds fascinating. Toys like this are eminently suitable for older cats whose movement is restricted for whatever reason.

Home-made obstacle course

A day in the life of a cat consists of long rest periods punctuated by bouts of activity. While an indoor cat spends most of the day sleeping, grooming himself, and feeding, cats who can go outside get up to much more, roaming their territory, climbing trees, exploring, meeting other cats, and hunting, during which time they will cover, on average, 8000-10,000m². Indoor cats have to be content with the confines of their owner's house; typically an area of 35-120m², although they still exhibit the same behaviours as their free-roaming peers: hiding and watching, exploring and hunting.

These activities play a significant role in the wellbeing of every cat. For the purposes of home entertainment, provide your cat with hidey-holes, resting areas, viewing platforms, and scratching posts to create the perfect playground for him. Apart from hunting

From a safe hiding place, she can observe human activity without being disturbed.

Through the opening ...

 Fun and games for cats!

Checklist for your cat tree

- ❏ Adapted to the specific needs of young, active animals, or older animals who may have poor health

- ❏ Attractive design

- ❏ Right kind of materials – nothing potentially toxic

- ❏ Is stable and balanced with one or more cats on it

- ❏ Colourfast leather, textiles, sisal, etc

- ❏ High quality workmanship

- ❏ Height adjustable and easily mounted ceiling attachment

- ❏ Several places to sit, including high-rise platforms

- ❏ Customer service available after you have purchased the product

- ❏ Spare parts available, warranty

- ❏ Can be erected without additional tools (self-assembly)

- ❏ Toys attached, such as mice or balls on a string

- ❏ Slip-resistant

- ❏ Durable

- ❏ Weatherproof (outdoor models)

... and quickly on to the cat tree. Shall I jump up onto the next platform or play with the mouse below?

Fun and games for cats!

A

B

C

A Loosen up
Benco is ready for his agility lesson

B Down we go
Making the leap from the upper level of the cat tree

C Neat landing
The front paws stretch outward and the hind legs are tucked into the body

D Athlete
A toy with a catnip scent – attached to the door – could give rise to an impressive athletic performance

E Balancing act
During enthusiastic climbing exercises, the tail helps him to keep his balance

D

E

games that you can play together with your cat (see page 54), it is essential you give him an adequate fitness area so he is able to enjoy himself and use any excess energy.

Cat activity trees

The essential needs and wants of a cat, such as climbing, claw-sharpening, hiding, and observing, can be provided by a cat tree, or activity tree. Think of it as a substitute for real trees, balcony railings and roofs, where cats love to practice their acrobatic and balancing skills, and keep a look-out for what's going on around them. Not only that, they are also handy as a place to sleep, and are used for sharpening claws, which will save your furniture time and time again. In order to appeal, these are your cat's criteria:

The cat tree should have several levels, with an elevated vantage point that offers a good overview of the area. Cats live for the third dimension: if the cat tree is near a window or patio door, he has full view of the outside. This increases his space, at least visually, and he can watch the neighbour's cat or the birds flying around.

The scratching post must be well-equipped with a solid base, so that it does not wobble or tip over when your cat jumps or moves around on it. If the cat has a bad experience with the scratching post because it doesn't hold his weight and suddenly tilts, he will become wary of his tree, and, instead, use the furniture for climbing on and sharpening claws. Cloth or sisal-covered poles, or even real tree trunks, are great for feline manicures, and hanging ropes tempt the cat to swing and climb.

Activity trees are available to buy in most pet shops, and many come with scratching posts, tunnels, and other elements. Even cat trees made from real logs are available. Many cats favour sisal-covered posts which offer several different levels of platform. For the creative DIY experts among

Checklist for solitary games

These toys will help your puss pass the time when on his own:

❏ Several mice (made from fake fur, cloth or other material depending on your cat's preference)

❏ Little balls, eg ping-pong balls

❏ Everyday objects suitable for cats such as corks, nuts, etc

❏ A snack ball and small pieces of dried food

❏ Cat activity tree

❏ Things to hide in (cardboard boxes, blankets, bags, etc)

❏ Cat tracks (a cat game where you can send balls rattling down tunnels and tracks)

❏ Toys with catnip scent

Kit bits

I SPY WITH MY LITTLE EYE …

Cats can see very well, even in minimal light, and are therefore very good at exploring dark places. At dusk, cats can see six times better than humans, though in total darkness, cats' eyes cannot perceive anything.

you, there are no limits – you can design a completely unique climbing world. Remember that the higher the climbing tree, the larger the base should be. You could also add a ceiling support for extra security.

Acrobat

Cats can prance through branches and balcony railings, or jump from roof to roof with excellent body control, demonstrate lightning-quick reactions, and have a keen sense of balance. The cat's tail serves as a balancing aid and provides excellent co-ordination. When it comes to climbing and jumping, cats are experts. Lightweight and fast, they can climb up tree trunks, their sharp claws dug into the bark and pushing upward with their powerful hind legs. The descent is more difficult, because cats claws don't give any support when upside down, so the climb down is done gently in reverse gear, or else the cat may courageously jump from a great height.

Cats possess an innate ability to orient and right themselves as they fall in order to land on their paws, and are able to twist to face the right way without changing momentum. They do this by bending in the middle, so that the front half of the body rotates about a different axis than the rear half. Then they tuck their front legs in to decrease front-end momentum, whilst extending the hind legs to increase rear-end momentum.

Wild, enthusiastic jumping from a great height is usually reserved for young or very active cats. Older animals who have problems with their joints are difficult to motivate to play a particularly physical game, as jumping often causes them pain. A change in diet and an individually tailored fitness programme can help an overweight cat to have more fun when exercising.

Catnip – a frenzy of the senses

Catnip (*Nepeta cataria*) contains the essential oils and substances nepetalacton and actinidin, to which many cats are magically drawn. While catnip (catmint) does not exude a fragrance that's unusual to the human nose, it can affect cats quite dramatically by sending

Even the impressive Leon forgets the world around him when he's got his paws on a catnip mouse.

Whether twitching toes or wiggly spaghetti, when at play, the attentive Lisa misses nothing,

them into a frenzy, triggering a variety of different behaviours.

After the catnip has been sniffed and licked, the cat may rub his chin and cheeks on it, and appear as if in a trance. A toy filled with catnip may be subjected to several blows from his strong paws. Since cats become very lively, playful, and curious after a taste of catnip, dried catnip leaves are often used as a filling for cushions or toy mice, and are an ideal way to rejuvenate tired or bored domestic tigers. For indoor cats, catnip is an effective way of making toys and scratching posts more interesting. However, not all cats show a reaction to catnip. Whether or not cats react to catnip scent is thought to be determined by genetics. Kittens under three months tend to show no interest in it.

Catnip cat

Toys, such as that shown on page 34 can be hung on the scratching post or from door handles. The smell of the catnip herb and the rustling noises of the toy will excite the cat, and motivate him to play. Cats love to hunt and pounce, especially with these sorts of toys, and can be easily encouraged to make high leaps to catch the prey.

Undercover mission

Cats love hidey-holes: they can watch all that goes on from a safe place without being discovered! The most popular hiding places are tunnels, drawers, or under a bed. Large cardboard boxes, with entrance and exit holes cut into them, are ideal hiding places also. Tissue paper or unrolled streamers make a

great rustling noise, and are terrific for chasing and pouncing on.

Tunnels

Toy tunnels are perfect for cats who like to hide. Inside, the hidden cat can take a nap, or play to his heart's content. The tunnel offers excitement, variety and adventure, and is available in different materials – some have a rustly material sewn inside, whilst others have multiple exits and dangling toy mice, balls, or little felt fish. You could create a multiple tunnel system, hide some toy mice inside, and send your agent on a secret 'undercover mission.'

A cat-wrap
A rolled-up rug makes an excellent hiding place

B Well camouflaged
The motto here is 'See but don't be seen'

C Stalker
A toy is produced and arouses the interest of the cat, who is mesmerised by his prey

D Tunnel
Cats are magically drawn to small hideaways like this

E Look-out duty
Hiding, exploring, and observing are instinctive behaviours for every cat

Playmates & best buddies

In the company of cat playmates, life is much more varied. Chases, exciting brawls, playing games, and hunting for mice is twice as much fun with a cat buddy

Loner or team-player?

The way cats live reflect their individuality and their incredible ability to adapt to different conditions. The fact that they are so independent often gives the impression that they are solitary creatures, averse to socialising with other cats. On the one hand, they can spend hours on their own in meadows and fields; on the other, they can live in social groups of various sizes and in different social structures. The richer the food supply in a particular area, the larger the cat colony.

Within the colony, matriarchal family ranking is recognised, and the animals maintain different social relationship networks, showing respect to their elders and playing with their peers. In the case of indoor cats, we humans have a significant impact on the social life of the cat because we determine whether they live alone or with a fellow cat (or other species of animal).

Many cats are kept alone and never have the opportunity to show that they are actually very sociable by nature.

Although the social life of cats is very complex, and requires some knowledge on the owner's part in order to have two or more cats living together harmoniously, don't let this put you off getting a buddy for your cat! What could be better than spending the day with his best friend while his master or mistress is out or at work?

Cuddly cat or game freak?
Through selective breeding, different breeds

Despite her imposing appearance, this Maine Coon is a gentle, sociable cat.

tend to have different characteristics, both physical and personality-wise. Persian cats are often described as peaceful and quiet, while Siamese cats are regarded as bright and very vocal. But, of course, there are exceptions.

Docile and endearing: Persian, Birman, Chartreux, British Shorthair, Exotic Shorthair, Ragdoll ...

Lively: Maine Coon, Norwegian Forest Cat ...

Temperamental: Siamese, Burma, Burmilla, Korat, Abyssinian, Turkish Angora, Singapura, Bengal, Somali, Balinese, Oriental Shorthair ...

And in a category of its own: the domestic short-haired cat.

kitten look like? What character traits will she inherit from her parents?

Catch me!

Running and catching activities are usually played by young or very active cats. In a wild chase, the kitten races back and forth across the room, over beds and chairs, on shelves and other furniture. Quickly, however, the roles

Birmans are considered to be calm and balanced companions.

Siamese cats are always ready for a game or two!

Domestic cats

The largest proportion of all felines are probably domestic cats. While the essential characteristics of pedigree cats are a little more predictable, the domestic short-haired cat is like a surprise package. What will the

change and the hunter becomes the hunted, and vice versa. This very athletic performance requires not only physical fitness and quick reactions, but also a lot of energy. However, it won't be long before the cat is lying on the sofa once again, recharging his batteries!

Top left: Young, active cats love to play hide and seek

Above: Fragile items should be moved out the way!

Left: The bowl didn't survive the game and the remains will now have to be investigated ...

Kit bits
THE NEED FOR COMPANIONSHIP

The need for companionship varies from cat to cat, and also depends on the different experiences he has had. If your cat is not as youthful as he once was, he may become grumpy with any outsiders he is unused to.

Kit bits
CHARACTERISTICS

The traits of a cat can be as varied and diverse as that of the human character. The genetic legacy of the parents, life experiences, learning processes, and preferences all have an influence on the personality of the animal, as well as the living environment.

It's not always easy to determine the temperament of a cat. Some are gentle, others extroverted and very vocal, or a little shy, but they can also be prickly and grouchy!

If your cat loves tearing around the house, open all the inner doors to create a race track. To ensure that nothing gets broken during the racing games, remove vases and other fragile objects from the 'track' area.

Hideaway
Hiding is often a feline favourite. Cartons, boxes, shopping bags, drawers, and shelves draw cats like a magnet. Once inside, they feel protected, watching everything and everyone without being seen. And if a fellow cat comes strolling along, your cat could pounce on him and set off a chase or a fighting game.

However, many cosy nooks in the

Shopping bags are a favourite hiding place for cats of all ages.

Catnip cushions are a popular prey, usually closely guarded.

house can turn out to be quite dangerous. Particularly popular are bags, and in the case of shopping bags, there's a danger that your four-legged friend could become entangled and eventually suffocate. If you let your puss play hiding games in bags, make sure you supervise him and cut off the bag handles. Paper bags are safer than plastic bags. Also, wardrobes or drawers can be a danger for cats, particularly if they are trapped inside whilst their owner is out.

Aim high

Cats love to watch their territory from above. In addition to ideal vantage points, a cat tree has much more to offer. Jumping, climbing, patting the hanging toys, or just having a rest. If you have more than one cat, you should make sure that each animal has his own area. Clashes over coveted places are inevitable!

In addition to the cat tree viewing platforms, shelves are bound to be a favourite for your acrobatic kitty as he winds his way between vases and ornaments. Make sure you remove any fragile items from the shelves, especially if you have a young or very active cat.

Cat fight

Fighting games are part of everyday life for adolescent cats. Threatening posture, attacking with a bite to the neck, and different battle and hunting techniques are all playfully experimented with. Cats love to execute delightfully playful attacks on their comrades, preferably from somewhere high up. Scuffling around and bellowing at one another are fun and very popular, and the game can be seriously fast and hard to keep up with at times.

Unimpeded social games are important for kittens because they are essential to personality development. Try not to interfere when your young, spirited moggies tumble through the house. The games probably look wilder than they actually are.

Overstepping the boundaries

It's not only adolescent cats who sometimes go too far in a fighting game – adult animals can also run into trouble. You should intervene in such confrontations only in cases where serious injury could occur, for example, biting. If one of the two animals appears to be attacking the other, you may feel inclined to punish the attacker and cosset the victimised cat, but this will have a negative effect on the friendship of the two animals. Such measures also affect your human-animal relationship.

Never back a cat into a corner, and always leave him an escape route. If you are trying to distract one of the two cats, don't do this by petting them or giving them treats, because you could thereby reinforce the aggressive behaviour. Instead, attract their attention by dropping something behind your back such as a keychain or a book. After the unexpected crash, the battle should stop because the animals will have been momentarily distracted. Sometimes, all it takes is a light shower from a water spray bottle to separate the two fighting cats – but make sure the spray bottle is on a fairly gentle setting!

Dancing feathers

Cats love feathers, especially when they move as if by magic. 'Catch Me' is a toy equipped with a motor and a remote control. The engine whirls the toy round and round, which stimulates the feline hunting instinct and provides great entertainment.

'Catch Me' is recommended not just for

The young cat dares to get too close to the scented pouch and gets a nasty surprise.

improved during this exercise. Once that feather starts moving about on the hook, the cat will be mesmerised. This game is also ideal for two or three cats at once.

The activity level of each cat is different, so tailor games to each individual feline. Anxious cats may often be dominated or excluded by confident, active cats; if this is the case, you should play in a group (in addition to playing with each animal individually), and ensure that none of the cats is left out of the game. As well as expending excess energy, the shy cat will feel more confident when you are all playing together, which, in turn, will help to strengthen the friendship between the animals.

Treasure hunt

Cartons and boxes offer excellent play potential for cats, so don't just chuck them away but convert them into a whole new world of adventure for your puss; the larger and more stable the box or carton, the better.

Cut holes in the box to make entrances and exits, and maybe even a few windows. Make the adventure even more exciting with rustling tissue paper, so he can hide in the box and have a great time playing with the paper. You could also hide a toy mouse or catnip pouches under the paper and encourage your cat to hunt for them.

This sort of game has the added benefot of being free or low-cost, and should appeal to all cats in your household. Put away the box after a few days once it becomes too familiar, presenting it two to three weeks later so that the fun can start all over again.

solo animals but also two or more cats. Not only does it improve physical fitness, but the animal's mental flexibility is also challenged. Due to the unpredictability of the game, motivation and interest tend to last longer. Cat owners can get the feather moving by using a remote control.

Prey on a string

Patting and reaching for prey is an ideal way to stimulate a cat's hunting instinct. Speed, fitness, and reaction times can all be greatly

A cardboard box can be a great adventure, and is an exciting experience for kittens.

Checklist: playing with other cats

Two or more cats can pass the time playing together with these toys:

- ❏ Several toy mice (fur, cloth, etc, depending on your cats' preference)

- ❏ Little balls

- ❏ Suitable everyday objects for cats to play with such as corks, cotton reels, etc

- ❏ Cat tree

- ❏ Hiding places (boxes, bags, etc)

- ❏ Cat turbo track (see http://www.discountedpetproducts.net/BLI_TOY_CAT_TURBO_TRACK-UKP129700.html

- ❏ Objects/toys scented with catnip

- ❏ Motor-operated cat toys ('Catch Me')

Fun and games for cats!

'Catch me!'

BASICS

A

B

A Is it alive?
Moving objects stimulate the prey drive and motivate cats to hunt

B Pat–pat
Once the desire to hunt has been aroused, the cat turns his full attention to his prey

C Changing direction
Co-ordination and quick reflexes are required. Suddenly, the feather escapes in an abrupt change of direction

D Almost got it
With a well-aimed strike of the paw and open mouth, he is trying to catch the feather. Much skill and dexterity is called for here

C

D

E Free-wheeling
Cats who are allowed outside spend up to six hours a day hunting, but indoor cats must satisfy their hunting instincts by playing games

F Again and again
Meggy can't get enough of this game!

G Attack!
She launches an attack

H Intensity
Matters can become tense in hunting games

I Total concentration
'Catch me' ensures that the cat will have to make many attempts before the prey is finally caught

Play with me!

Play-time between cats and their owners is really something special. It's great fun, and strengthens the bond between you and your pet. Exciting games and activities have the magical effect of turning a bored house cat into a happy and more fulfilled companion

Cats love to play!

Cuddly though they may sometimes be, our cats are still predators, whose favourite pastime is hunting. While cats who can go outside use up a lot of energy when hunting, indoor cats are more reliant on their humans to provide them with play opportunities. They spend a significant part of the day sleeping, grooming themselves and eating, while their free-roaming counterparts spend about six to eight hours a day hunting and exploring their outdoor territory.

Outdoor substitute

In the wild, an animal's chances of survival are increased by his ability to learn from experience. Since indoor cats are denied this type of training, the daily play routine with their owner is vitally important to them. If the needs of the animal are not met through exercise and mental stimulation, this can result in behavioural problems. Some domestic tigers are very inventive in their quest to dissipate pent-up energy: in the absence of a more suitable object, stalking his owner's legs or feet makes a great alternative prey. It's not unusual for a cat to wake his owners from sleep just because 'poor puss' is bored. Even more reason, then, to keep your cat occupied during waking hours!

Prey on a string

There are loads of cat toys which replicate 'prey,' such as a toy mouse or a feather attached to a rod or a piece of string or ribbon. You could also easily make a toy like this

Kit bits
MOOD BAROMETER

Play can be used as an indicator of the wellbeing of an animal. Cats that are under stress don't play as often, or may stop playing altogether.

yourself by attaching a piece of string to a long stick (don't use rubber bands because of the risk of injury), then tying a toy to the other end of the string. Toys suitable for this purpose

Knowing what makes your cat tick means you can choose the correct toy for him, which will make all the difference to the success of the hunt. Also, don't forget that practice makes perfect.

are furry mice, balls, small stuffed animals or feathers, corks, and empty cotton reels.

As long as it moves

Anything that moves and can be 'killed' is extremely exciting for cats. As mentioned above, toys on play-rods are well suited to stimulating the prey instinct, and also provide animal and human with a great game to play together. Speed, fitness, and lightning-quick reactions are required on the part of the huntress, while the human must show commitment to the game and empathy for the cat.

You will need to mimic the prey in a way that doesn't alarm your cat. Firstly, the object of desire must be the right size: most cats will respond to small-sized toys and shy

To maintain a slimline figure, regular physical exercise for neutered indoor cats is a must. Help your moggy maintain his washboard stomach!

away from larger ones. An object the size of a mouse is perfect. And in the case of feathers, the more impressive these are, the greater the cat's desire to hunt.

Realistic prey

Another important factor is movement. The 'prey' has to hide, flee, hop, twitch and fidget, or it won't seem real. Move the toy mouse or similar object away from your cat and not toward him. If you have a cat play-rod with ribbons attached, for example, twist and wind it around like a snake, or make a feather-toy 'fly' through the air. Basically, anything that moves away from him and flies, crawls, wriggles, jumps or rolls, will spur on the hunt. However, waving the toy too wildly in front of

your cat's face will irritate him, spoil the fun, and could be perceived as a possible attack.

Play-rods are a great way to have fun with your cat. Feathers are the most popular attachment because they are the perfect replacement for a real bird. When the play-rod is moved about, the feathers at the end of the string will make a fluttering noise. An added bonus is that, with most of these toys, the feathers can be replaced. When the tuft of feathers dance on the end of the play-rod, kitty will be beside herself with excitement, and attempt to hook the feathers with her claws. Less active cat owners can play this game while sitting on the sofa, while the sporty ones amongst you can race through the house, with your moggy hot on your heels!

Kit bits
CATS' EYES

Feline eyes are especially attuned to the perception of movement and distance – allowing for rapid fixation on their prey, even at a distance, although motionless objects are harder for him to discern.

Magic wand

Play-rods come in many variations, such as ones with ribbons or feathers attached at the end, or plush balls with catnip scent. These types of play-rod are ideal for interactive games between human and cat, and you can settle yourself comfortably on the sofa and play with your moggy. Many cats, especially shy ones, will love to paw at the toy while hiding – on top of the cat-tree, on a shelf or other hiding place. Also, it's especially fun when the ball disappears under a blanket or a rug, which means that the 'invisible' prey can be hunted down and caught.

In research studies involving several cats at once, balls filled with catnip herbs proved to be the cat toy of choice. This toy not only motivates the moggy to hunt, it's also a great way to improve his fitness.

Long-fingered glove

During hunting games, human fingers are at risk of being mistaken for prey. This glove, with extra long fingers and pom-poms at the tips, is ideal because it allows enough distance between the hand and kitty's claws. The fingers of the glove are quite thick and flexible, so they can be moved by your own fingers. Some pet shops sell gloves with colourful fabric insects at the ends of the fingers.

Not all cats will take to this toy. Shy or timid animals need some time to get used to it, and will appreciate being able to examine and sniff the glove in peace before the game

Fully focused, the cat attempts to catch the flying object ...

... with claws extended, the prey is caught.

Great fun! Let's do it again!

begins. Since the 'fingers' are reinforced with wire, and the pom-poms are attached to rubber bands, during the game special care should be taken; ensure there are no wires protruding which may injure your cat, and don't give him the opportunity to chew on the rubber bands. Once the game has ended, put the glove away.

Cat Dancer ®

At first glance, the Cat Dancer ® toy from the US seems rather unimpressive: a flexible spring steel wire that is attached to some rolled-up cardboard. However, if you hold the wire loosely between your fingers, it floats up and down. Move the toy, make it dance a little, and it makes a noise like buzzing insects, caused by the rolled cardboard vibrating against the springs. Watch your puss jump around with the toy and show off his best acrobatic moves! Because of the steel wire, it must be stored safely after use (http://www.catdancer.com/).

This toy is filled with catnip and material that rustles.

The reinforced fingers are flexible, and there are four pom-pom balls at the tips for added attraction.

After the cat has played and worn himself out, he looks forward to cuddle time with his owner. He knows what's good for him!

Cat sport

Indoor cats are simply not as active as their outdoor counterparts, and also have less variety in everyday life, so many of them eat out of boredom. Therefore, you will need to encourage your moggy to move a bit more. Cats who are very active stay in shape and are less likely to have a weight problem. So, you can kill two birds with one stone by playing with your cat, which will prevent him from becoming bored, and also help him to lose weight. In addition, you will strengthen his muscles, improve his physical fitness and co-ordination, and relieve everyday stress. Would

you like to try a workout session à la cat? Then sit cross-legged on the floor, feather toy in your hand, and let's go!

Get into the game slowly by starting with a warm up lap. Play sessions should last no longer than 10-15 minutes, tailored according to your pet's abilities and condition. Cats love prey games, so you could change the object or vary the game; tempt your little tiger and then let him catch the spoils after a few goes. If your cat shows signs of fatigue or loses interest, you should end the game. Ideally, you should finish the game slowly, before he stops enjoying it. In practice, this

Fun and games for cats!

Top: From the chair, the feathers can easily be batted with both paws.

Middle: The prey disappears under the chair ... as does the cat, head first.

Bottom: As the feathers dance around the chair legs, the wild hunt begins.

means that the toy slows down, until you stop the movement and thus the game. This is also the best way to say 'game over' if you've had enough. Cats are sensitive creatures who can perceive your moods and assess whether or not you are enthusiastic about what you're doing.

Round and round

Show your cat that you have a toy and move it slowly away from him. Make it disappear behind your back, and then reappear on the other side of you. By now, the hunting instinct of your moggy should be aroused and you can really get into the game. To warm up your cat, make a circle around your body with the

The feathers play-rod whirling across the floor will bring even the shyest cat out of her shell.

A Warm up
Any sporting activity should always begin with a warm up. Willow runs under her owner's legs as part of hers

B Get going
This is followed by a chase, ensuring that she can't quite reach the feathers

C & D Leaps and bounds
The activity increases pace, the acrobatics become more daring. Moves include high jumps typical of those which feral cats use when hunting prey

E Cool down
After 10 minutes or so, slowly end the game. Allow your cat to catch the prey and then let her rest

With great enthusiasm, the table tennis ball is skilfully caught. Maybe he should play professionally!

toy that your cat can follow. Then drag the toy under your legs, which are drawn up to allow him to crawl through the 'tunnel.' Especially athletic cats may jump on your legs, sit up and beg for the toy, or show off their best acrobatic skills. When kitty is tired, put him on your lap for a cuddle break!

Take a rest

After such intensely athletic games, it's time for a rest period. Most cats prefer the evening hours for wild games, so you can have a few spirited rounds of play, and then cuddle and grooming time. How about a massage for your athlete? If you massage him with gentle fingertips over the head, ears and back, he is bound to purr. Or perhaps your feline friend would rather have a snack from the food bowl first, and then find a cosy spot to rest.

Slalom skiers

Young cats are especially active and full of energy, which is definitely a requirement for this exercise. Use a play-rod to encourage your pet to perform this intensive exercise.

Place a chair in the middle of the room and encourage your cat to jump onto the seat by attracting him with the play-rod. He should start boxing the toy, to warm up, so to speak. Then move the play-rod up and down the chair legs, and make it disappear under the seat. It will not be long until your cat turns upside down after the prey, and then jumps to the ground. Then, imagine the chair legs are the poles between which he has to run. Move the play-rod between the chair legs in a figure of eight, or back and forth. If your cat makes himself comfortable in the chair, you should stop the exercise. And don't forget to let him catch the prey at the end of the game, because that makes kitty happy and motivated for the next game.

Cat football
This requires a good level of fitness.

Cats love it when their owner is at the same eye level as them. Get on the floor, or for those who find this too uncomfortable, the game can be played sitting on the bed or the sofa. Have your cat stand in front of a wall or in the corner of a room, as if he is a goalie. Now roll the ball towards the 'goal.' Your goalkeeper will capture the ball at lightning speed and keep it, or if you're lucky, he may bat it back to you. You will be amazed at how cleverly your cat can calculate the exact path of the ball – managing to get it past him will be quite difficult!

Squash for top athletes
Some breeds, such as Siam, Burma, or Maine Coon, are among the best feline athletes, and would definitely benefit from a sporting challenge or two. To play Cat squash, repeatedly bounce a rubber ball on the ground, or throw it against the wall while your cat is trying to capture it. This gives active animals an opportunity to burn off energy and hone their co-ordination skills.

Catch me!
Many cats love to play tag and hide-and-seek. You'll know when he's begging

Even lying down, a cat has a good chance of catching the ball.

Fun and games for cats!

A Hidden treasure
A catnip mouse hidden under an old towel will never go unappreciated by any cat

B Excavation
With skill and stamina, she tries to get to the prize

C Sharp claws
Now she lifts the towel, using her claws

D A real treasure
Alternatively, a chain of wooden beads makes a fantastic rattling noise under the towel

E Exhausting
Demands on her mental energy can tire out even the liveliest cat

you to play because he'll gallop past you, his body side-on to you and his tail raised high in the air, calling upon his human to join in the pursuit. Allow him a head start: don't outrun him and don't find your kitty in his hiding place immediately. Or turn the tables and chase your cat around the apartment. Exercise not only burns fat and improves endurance, it also helps digestion and speeds up metabolism as well.

Flying carpet
Hunting and touch games with an unseen prey hold a special charm for our feline friends. His paws can feel for an object underneath something else, or he can feel movement but he can't see the prey. This

makes it more of a challenge, because he must reveal the hidden treasure.

There are lots of variations of this game. Place a small rug or a runner on the floor and put a large, smooth stone underneath it; tie a cork on a string and pull it slowly under a blanket, or hide a catnip mouse under a towel ... let your imagination run wild!

Cats are creatures of habit, and will often focus totally on a particular toy.

Checklist: Rules for kids

How to have fun with your cat:

- ❏ Cats are not toys. Treat your cat with respect and love

- ❏ Cats generally do not like rough and noisy games

- ❏ Never pull her tail or fur. It will hurt your cat and she may defend herself with her claws

- ❏ If your cat is asleep, don't wake her to play

- ❏ After eating, your cat needs to rest, after which you can play with her

- ❏ Don't look her straight in the eye; cats find this threatening. When looking at her, blink plenty of times so that your gaze doesn't worry her

- ❏ Marbles and small toys can be swallowed by your cat or become stuck in her throat. Tidy away your toys so that your bedroom is always cat-friendly

- ❏ If your cat suddenly no longer wants to play and turns away, then the game is over

- ❏ If you want to stroke your cat, wait until your game is finished. If you stroke her while playing, she may mistake this for part of the game and scratch you by mistake

Cats and children

There are so many exciting things for cats to play with in children's bedrooms. Balls, ribbons and small toys are easy targets for nimble paws, and are soon squirreled away. Plastic figures which are not too small or too big can be arranged in a kind of obstacle course for the cat. You could also try hiding some dry food in amongst all the toys for kitty to find. Don't forget to deduct these additional morsels from the daily ration, or puss might get fat!

Cats enjoy playing with children, but it's important that the children have learned a few rules for when interacting with any animal. By playing together, the relationship between child and cat will be strengthened. Please don't forget, however, that games between children and animals should always be supervised by an adult.

Play it safe

Check toys for your cat with the same care that you would for your child. There are a lot of things in a child's bedroom that can be dangerous for cats. Make sure that toys used for playing with the cat are a certain size, and thus cannot be swallowed, or become stuck in his throat. Rubber bands, wool, marbles, broken balloons, modelling clay, sharp objects, or the like are off-limits to cats. Explain to your child what to look for when choosing the right object for the cat to play with.

Play ideas from everyday life

Do you love to treat your cat to new toys? Then take a look at everything in your home through the eyes of your cat. You're bound to discover some interesting new toys which are perfect for cats – and completely free as well!

What's that rustling noise?

There's something in the box ...

You need a big box, tissue paper or streamers, and a toy mouse. Choose a box that is in proportion to the size of your cat. Cut circular or rectangular openings in the box, whichever you prefer, for windows, entrances and exits. Cover the bottom of the box with crumpled tissue paper, and hide the mouse under a couple of layers of this. Alternatively, you can cover the bottom of the box with unrolled paper streamers and bury the little mouse in the pile of paper.

The rustling sounds and hidden objects appeal to a cat's sense of touch, and will motivate him to hunt. Your cat can also hide away in the box or pounce on his cat buddies!

Make sure the openings in the box don't have sharp edges so your cat doesn't hurt himself. Fruit crates are also ideal hideaways. Once your cat is fed up of hunting the mouse, the box serves as a very comfortable place for him to sleep.

Mystery boxes

Any size box will do – even a small shoebox can be used for an exciting fishing game. Cut small holes in the side walls and small openings in the lid (use a large egg cup as a template so that you can draw neat circles and then cut them out). The holes should be large enough for your cat to comfortably fit his paws into and fish for toys. Fill the box with his favorite toys, such as mice, balls,

etc, then let your cat put his paw skills to the test!

Tissue balls

Not only does tissue paper make interesting rustling noises to entertain your cat, you can also shape it into balls. The feather-light balls can be nudged with your foot or tossed in the air, and are a simple but effective way to keep puss busy and occupied.

Cut the tissue paper into A5- or A4-sized sheets. Crumple the sheets into small balls, throw them to your cat – and watch the

The kitten is king of the box. He is nice and cosy, and can survey his surroundings in comfort.

A box and a crumpled piece of paper. Minimum effort, maximum fun – it'll keep your cat amused for hours!

Kit bits
CAT PAWS

Cats are very adept when it comes to getting into small cracks and holes to catch mice. A cat's toes are very flexible – if the object of desire is stuck, he can grip it with his toes and claws and pull it out. The sheathing mechanism ensures that the claws are protected and remain sharp and ready for action. In addition, he has pacinian corpuscles in his paw pads – tiny sensory organs which respond to touch – and can detect even the smallest shocks and vibrations in the ground.

fun begin as he chases and bats the balls. Another option is to fold a sheet of tissue paper in half and hide a small piece of dry food or a cat toy between the two halves. This will keep your cat busy until the tissue paper lies in tatters and the loot is recovered.

Goody bags
Cats love paper bags, big or small, and regardless of their appearance. Bags rustle, and are wonderfully suited for hunting and hiding.

Use a paper bag without handles or remove the handles yourself to prevent your cat becoming tangled or injured. Now, put a mouse or a catnip pouch into the bag and move it slightly back and forth. Your moggy's

Fun and games for cats!

Balls of crumpled tissue paper are simple to make, inexpensive, and popular toys for every cat. Your cat can catch them, pat them around or tear them apart – great fun!

Hidden in amongst all the paper, the mouse is still conspicuous to the cat ...

... and has aroused his hunting instinct.

The prey is just about to be caught.

curiosity is quickly aroused, and he'll be longing to see what's in the bag. Put some toys in the bag, then fold over the top, or twist it so that your cat can't see into it. Now, let's see how long that paper bag lasts!

Some animals have more fun with the packaging of something than the content (just like children!). For others, the interior of each bag is the most exciting bit. However, once you have encouraged your cat to hunt in bags, don't be surprised if he pokes his nose where it's not wanted; for example, the shopping bag with his owner's new silk blouse inside …! Store any bags you don't want him climbing into somewhere cat-proof. Remember, your cat can't distinguish between permitted and forbidden bags.

Simply scent-sational

It's not just dogs who love to smell, cats also love different scents. Scent-marking with urine or faeces provides information to and from other cats, and where they are; flower and herb perfumes delight a cat's nose, and the scent of prey arouses the desire to hunt. While cats who are allowed outside can gather new scent messages daily, indoor cats must depend upon a well-known and limited environment.

Perfume boxes

An indoor cat's environment is usually not very varied, and different visual and scent experiences are often quite limited. You could provide him with a little more variety by bringing home fragrant souvenirs depending on the season.

For example, in the autumn, put out a potpourri box of colourful leaves and chestnuts: he will love patting and chasing the chestnuts across the floor. Acorns, pine cones, pieces of wood or stones will also be thoroughly investigated by your cat. Many cats are also fascinated by wild herbs and love to smell flowers.

Many plants are toxic to pets, so check in advance whether the plants are safe for animals. On the Internet, there's a website that lists and describes those plants which are dangerous to cats: http://www.moggies. co.uk/plants.html

Outdoor scents

It's incredibly exciting for your puss when you come home with new scents on you. All the smells that you have picked up on your skin and clothing along the way are interesting to her, and bring the wide world back into her home territory. You've probably already noticed that your cat sniffs you extensively when you return home, and peeks into the shopping basket with great curiosity. Don't react negatively to her curiosity – allow her to sniff away to her heart's content. She will love teabags, herbs, or other small food packages. Hide a little toy mouse or a piece of dried food in the bag – that should intrigue her for a while!

Pillow talk

Cats spend a large part of the day sleeping, and love to curl up in places that they find restful and soothing. Spray a little cushion or pouch with some catnip. The heady scent may have a strange effect on your cat: she might roll from side to side, or nibble, lick and chew the cushion. Her face may take on an ecstatic look for the following ten or 15 minutes, and then Kitty is back to normal. You could also try filling a jute or hessian bag with catnip.

Actually, not all cats respond to the scent of catnip, which can occasionally have a negative effect on some animals, making them irritable and aggressive. If you notice this with your feline, remove the pouch and leave him in peace. To make the aroma of catnip pillows and mice last longer, put the toys in an airtight container and store in a cool, dark, dry place. Since your cat may salivate in ecstasy, you should select materials that are easy to

In contrast to indoor cats, cats who are allowed outside are in daily contact with a variety of odours and visual experiences.

clean, or machine washable. You could even spray a handkerchief or a scrap of material with catnip spray, which your cat can use as a sniffer-toy.

Sheer nosiness

Cats are endlessly fascinated by their environment, and seem to be curious about anything. My cats are all terribly curious, and investigate everything and everyone. How curious is your cat? Here's a quick test.

Throw a toy mouse inside a large pot, or kneel in front of the sofa and look interested in something you can see underneath. I bet it

won't be long until kitty comes to investigate! This is a simple game that requires no preparation, and which you can play any time. It will be a welcome hiatus to his routine.

Light games

Almost all cats love to watch small, quick-moving lights dancing on the floor or scurrying up the wall, for example, from a flashlight or

A box filled with colourful autumn foliage gives a cat access to a whole new fragrance. He might even be able to detect traces of other cats and animals ...

Many cats seem mysteriously drawn to fragrant flowers, therefore always check that yours aren't harmful to animals (see www.moggies.co.uk/plants.html).

torch. They love to hunt down the supposed prey, chasing after the light. Initially, the challenges of this game make it even more fun, but soon, the cat becomes disappointed when she realises that she cannot actually get hold of the light. Therefore, after getting her to chase the light back and forth, you should direct the beam of light at a toy or a treat and give your kitty a taste of success.

Note, though, that frantically moving the light back and forth can irritate your cat and spoil the fun, so don't make a joke out of this game by winding up your cat. The correct

way to play is to move the beam of light back and forth at an average pace, pausing to let it disappear behind the sofa, for example. Please ensure that you never shine the light directly into your cat's eyes. Laser pointers are a definite no-no in any circumstances, because a cat's eye can be damaged by the beam.

Paw training
Cats need challenges: they want to touch, test, grab, and reach. If a cat catches his prey straight away, where is the challenge? It's only

Tulips are toxic to cats. Smelling is allowed, but eating is forbidden!

Kit bits
SENSE OF SMELL

Compared to people, who have 5-20 million olfactory cells, cats have 60-65 million, so they are far more sensitive to odours. Even the lowest concentrations of odour-active molecules will attract a cat and get him sniffing. He will smell not only to detect prey, but also to forage for other food and establish contact with other cats and people. This highly developed sense is essential for hunting, orienteering, communication between individuals, and recognition of the whereabouts of other cats.

Once the desired prey is out of reach, the thrill of the chase soon wears off and is replaced by frustration.

Toy mice are made from many different materials. Each cat has a favourite type of mouse!

when he has to use his skills and his brain that the game begins to be interesting.

Pyramid play

For this game, you will need several empty toilet rolls or kitchen rolls, tissue paper, food treats, and toy mice or other small objects. Give your imagination free rein – be as creative as you like.

Glue together several empty rolls in a tower, a wall, or even a pyramid. If you enjoy making things, you could even paint the rolls with non-toxic paint, or cover them in different fabrics. Once the paint has dried, turn your attention to the inside of the rolls. Close some of the rolls with tissue paper, fill some with edible treats or a toy mouse, and leave the rest of the rolls empty.

Activities such as these require your cat to use his head and have fun, but won't take too much time or money to make. Filling the tubes with interesting objects or food will inspire your cat and encourage him to investigate. This is an ideal game for cats who are on their own during the day, or a great game to play with a team-mate. Be careful you don't slide the toys or food so far into the tube (particularly if it's a kitchen roll) that your cat can't reach them. Little by little, though, push the treats further and further into the tubes to increase the challenge.

Some cats will gently and quietly investigate the rolls, others may try to push them over or fling them around! If this is the case, you could glue the rolls onto a shoe box lid to ensure they stay in the right position.

Prey roll

For the prey roll, you need a kitchen towel roll, tissue paper, and small pieces of dried food or some treats. Cut a square hole in the middle of the tube that is slightly larger than the food morsels, and use tissue paper to close each end. Place the dried food inside. Your puss will be fascinated by the rattling as he rolls the tube back and forth and studies the opening. The first few treats that drop out of the opening will incentivise your cat to continue playing with the roll.

You can vary the difficulty of the game by blocking the hole in the tube with some more crumpled tissue paper. Kitty will then have to remove this in order to get to the treats.

Kit bits
THE CATS' WHISKERS

The whiskers on the upper lip, above the eyes, on the cheeks and chin are called vibrissae, and respond to the lightest of touches. They act as a guide in the dark, measure the width of holes and gaps, and signal to the cat the exact place on the prey to make that final, fatal bite. When the mouse is caught and taken back to the den, the whiskers tell the cat if the mouse is slipping away or if he has it firmly in his grasp.

Chocolate box
At some point, chocolates can be found in almost every household. Once the chocolates have been eaten, use the plastic tray from inside the box as a cat toy.

Fill some of the sections in the tray with dried food and let your cat fish them out. Even the cardboard box offers exciting possibilities: cut a hole in the lid, put some tissue paper inside, and hide a toy mouse with a bell on it

Skilled paws required: in this pyramid of senses, the cat can hunt and fish out objects from the various openings.

Fun and games for cats!

A

B

A Beginners
The first task should be simple and the prey easily accessible

B My treat
If the dried food is placed close to the openings, your moggy should achieve fast results

C Advanced
Here's something for the advanced player; hooking the kibble out of the cup

D Peek in the tunnel
The opening is just big enough to take a look and sample with a paw

E Slow but sure
A last, he gets the treat

C

D

E

amongst the paper. Once the lid is back on, shake the box so that your cat can hear the rustling noise – he'll soon be well away!

Surprise

Have you heard of Kinder Surprise? You may not buy these for yourself but maybe for one of your children, nieces, nephews or grandchildren? Popular with young children, these chocolate eggs have a little toy within a yellow container, which makes the perfect cat toy. Fill this with grains of uncooked rice or pasta, give it to the cat – and watch him go! The little plastic container can be pinged across the floor, or rolled back and forth with the paws.

For my cats, the Kinder Surprise is in the top ten favorite toys of all time. Especially popular is the version with a ribbon inside. Open the egg, tie a knot in the end of the ribbon, and trap the knotted end inside the container. You can now hang the 'punch bag' on a hook on the cat-tree, or from another suitable place. For safety reasons, don't allow your cat to play with this toy unsupervised.

Cat mobile

It's not only children who love mobiles – cats think it's great fun to pat a toy which is dangling right in front of their nose.

You need a couple of cords or ribbons, and some cat toys or other suitable household

The Kinder egg is popular with young children and very cheap. After the chocolate is eaten, the container can be transformed into a cat toy: little stones or grains of rice inside it will make a lovely, rattly noise.

Kit bits
NO CHOCOLATE!

Never give your cat human chocolate. It contains theobromine, which causes vomiting and diarrhoea in cats, which can be fatal.

Opposite, top: It wobbles, twists and turns ...

Middle: ... can be flung into the air ...

Bottom: ... and rattles when it moves. Perfect!

objects. Attach a mouse, a ball of tissue paper or a feather to each cord or ribbon. Then tie the mobile to the back of a chair. The chair should be heavy so that it doesn't tip over when the cat is playing with the mobile and swinging from the toys. If you hang the objects at different heights and have enough space between each object, your cat can get really involved and the game is more satisfying.

If the cat mobile is going to be a permanent fixture, ensure that the toys are securely fastened, and cannot be chewed off and swallowed by your cat. Remove any toys which require supervision when played with.

Water play

Cats are usually a water-shy species, but

Kit bits
Hertz frequencies

Humans can hear up to 20,000 Hz, but feline hearing capacity is superior by far. Cats can hear up to an incredible 70,000 Hz.

---

there are some 'water rats' who delight in any games involving water. Indoor fountains are not just good for interior design – they also improve the indoor climate. Just as the slow ripple of the fountain has a relaxing effect on humans, so cats are equally attracted by the sounds and movement of the water. A small

Cats are curious creatures, and even a bucket of water has to be carefully investigated. Perhaps there are fish there? Or maybe I can chase the drops of water?

Acoustic signals like rustling, scratching or squeaking noises grab a cat's attention and encourage him to search for prey.

rubber ball or a cork floating in water in a bucket could keep your pet busy for quite some time, but check that the bucket can't be pulled over.

Since cats like to drink from pots, buckets, etc, pay attention to hygiene and water quality. Don't use chemical additives in the water, for the sake of your pet's wellbeing. Many cats prefer drinking from a dripping or running water tap, and can spend quite some time at the sink in the kitchen. Your cat may like to watch the falling wate: droplets, chase after the drops, or even put his head under the tap.

Make sure that the water is neither too hot nor too cold.

Eavesdropping

Rustling, crackling, and squeaking sounds get the attention of every cat. No wonder, since cats' ears are very sharp so as not to miss even the quietest sounds made by a mouse, perfectly designed so that they can be moved independently, and directed toward a sound source.

Cats' ears are designed to hear high-frequency sounds, such as the noises made by small rodents. Attract your cat to a noise such as a toy mouse that squeaks or rustles, or by tapping your fingers on the tabletop. It is exciting for them to follow the source of the sound in their own territory and to explore

Fun and games for cats!

what is going on – and what their human is making such a fuss about. Some cats just love squeaky toy mice and will carry them round the house all day.

Rustly worm

You can make a great cat toy from an old pair of tights. Cut off a leg and fill it with scraps of paper, tissue paper and dried catnip. Then tie or sew the leg together at several points so that it is divided into small segments. Make sure that the sections of the 'worm' are not filled to bursting so that the objects inside each section can be moved by your cat. Remember: the best toys appeal to all senses – eyes, nose, ears, paws and claws are all required here!

This lattice ball – which is actually a dog toy – is ideal for investigative games.

Checklist: Caution, dangerous toys!

- ❏ Balls and other toys should be an appropriate size so that they cannot be accidentally swallowed, or become lodged in the throat

- ❏ The toy must not be sharp or splinter in the heat of the moment

- ❏ Broken toys should be discarded and replaced

- ❏ Do not use small, easy-to-swallow parts in toys (easily removable eyes on toy mice, or a small squeaker in a squeaky toy)

- ❏ Toys should be free from toxic paint and coatings

- ❏ Assess the suitability and chewability of each toy

- ❏ Beware of plastic bags, which represent a choking/suffocation hazard if your puss becomes tangled in it

- ❏ Never let your pet play with rubber bands, wool, rolled-up foil, needles, paper clips, tinsel, drawing pins, balloons, or similar

- ❏ Laser pointers are a complete no-no for cats

Intelligence games

Not only are our cats excellent athletes and hunters, they are also more than capable of puzzling out a problem. Give your moggy the chance to show off his brainpower – he'll love it!

Clever cats

Puzzling it over …

Most cat owners are in agreement that their four-legged friends have outstanding abilities, and are capable of amazing thought processes. There are cats who can open doors, break into packets of food, and find their way home from miles away. Cats know how to manipulate their owners, almost unconsciously. They can interpret our feelings, and know exactly what mood we're in; for

The cup game calls upon her sense of smell, and encourages Bibi to use her grey matter. She will need to figure out different strategies in order to get to the prey.

example, your cat might retreat from you when you're in a bad mood, or try and comfort you in sad times.

Look and learn

Cats learn by observation and imitation. Kittens watch their mothers in order to learn skills needed for everyday life, such as hunting, socialising with other cats, and using the litter tray to become house-trained. Adult cats often serve as a role model, and a young cat will quickly learn how the cat flap works, or how the cupboard door opens to reveal a coveted treat, from watching and copying a cat buddy.

Crafty but cute

For this game you need a few pieces of dried food and two plastic cups. Place the two cups just in front of your cat. Show her the treat and then hide it under one of the two cups. Kitty will look interested and immediately begin to try and uncover the delicacy. Very shy animals will most likely sniff the cups first, then self-consciously pat them with a paw, trying to knock over the container. Once your cat has

Bibi chooses the right cup ...

solved the problem and has the hang of what to do, you can increase the difficulty by hiding the treat under a cup when she is not looking. Remember to praise her whether she gets the treat straight away or takes a while to do so.

You should use lightweight plastic cups so that your cat is able to knock them over. You could try replacing the plastic cup with an empty yogurt pot, which increases the difficulty of the game. Don't forget to deduct the dry food from your cat's daily ration.

Centrifugal motion

For this task, you need a large plastic cup and a treat. Put the treat in the cup and tip it on

... and tips it over to get to the treat.

Trying to get to the treat when the cup is on its side is quite difficult because the cup moves like a spinning top, and is difficult for the animal to grip.

its side. If the cat pats the cup with his paw, it will spin like a top and make it harder for him to grab it. Some cats immediately know what to do and how to get the loot. This cat solved the problem within a few seconds: he stuck his paw in the cup and lifted it up. The treats tumbled out and were eaten.

Cup parade

Plastic cups can keep your moggy amused and on the go for quite some time. For this game, you will need different shaped pots: some have a wavy edge, so the cat can smell or see the treat, but others have straight edges so the cat has to lift it to see what's

Bibi puts her paw into the cup and lifts it.

Bibi has been paying attention and picks the cup with the treat underneath it.

Cats have a short concentration span, and need rest periods between exercises. Once rested, they will be more willing to try out new solutions, such as pushing the cup across the room.

Kit bits
COLOUR VISION

Contrary to popular belief, cats are not colour-blind, although colour vision seems to have only minor significance for cats.

underneath. To warm up, choose a cup, put the treat under it, making sure that your cat sees you, and then let him investigate. In the next round, set up three cups, and put a treat in each. Slowly increase the difficulty level by increasing the number of cups and reducing the number of treats. The kitty cup-connoisseur will be fascinated when you move the cups around in front of his eyes. See if he has noticed where the treat is hidden or whether he can smell the scent coming from the right cup.

Hunting for treats hidden underneath the cups is a difficult task for a cat. The cups are heavier than plastic cups or yogurt pots, and are all different shapes. The animal must use his brains and skill to resolve this puzzle.

Ping-Pong party
Table tennis balls are very popular with cats due to their characteristics: they are light and can be easily batted across the room with just one pat of the paw.

For this intelligence game, you'll need a shallow plastic container from the kitchen. Put one or two pieces of dried food in the base of the box, and add some table tennis balls. There should be sufficient space available to allow your cat to easily move the balls around and discover his treats under them.

Harder now
You can increase the difficulty level by filling a deeper box to the brim with table tennis balls. Now the cat has to dig to get to the treats. Prepared to be amazed at how efficiently your cat solves this puzzle!

Cats tend to really enjoy this game, which can be varied by changing the number

These balls are perfect for lots of different games.

A Pinpoint
An observant and attentive Bibi locates the treat

B Dig for it
In the hunt for the 'prey,' balls are pushed to one side or tossed out of the container

C The next level
A box with higher sides is more of a challenge

D Change of technique
Using her paws to try and fish out the balls doesn't appear to work ...

E Over she goes
Finally, Bibi realises what she must do and tips over the box – out roll the balls and the treat can be reached!

of table tennis balls, and also the size and shape of the container. This keeps the game exciting, and if all the treats are found, patting the Ping-Pong balls is great fun as well!

Open sesame!

A strong grip is required to open the lid of a container in order to reach the prey. In a plastic box with a lid, place a catnip pouch. Drawn by the enticing smell, your cat will try to find a gap with her paw, open the lid, and then stick her whole head in the box on top of the catnip pouch!

For difficult tasks, play sessions should last for only a few minutes, because cats generally have short attention spans. In each session, they should be allowed to capture their prey or receive a treat, as only then is the game successful for them. If this is not the case, they will soon lose interest. Help your cat with the task before he gives up.

Beware: this task will make your cat more dexterous, and so is more likely to begin opening boxes and packages that are not meant for him!

Best friend's toys

Do you live with a cat and a dog, perhaps? Then try out some dog toys with your cat. Many pet shops sell lattice balls in various sizes, so use a small- or medium-sized grid ball (see photo on page 86), depending on the toy you want to stash inside it. These special balls are light and flexible, and a cat can fit his whole paw through the openings and feel for the prey, almost as he would with a mouse hole.

All wrapped up

For this game, all you need is a towel and a toy; maybe a toy mouse with catnip scent, rustling tissue paper, or any other toy suitable for cats. You could use large wooden beads on a string, as they feel great through the material and will make a loud noise on a hard

The cat opens the box with his nose and head.

One paw holds the lid whilst the other grips the prey.

He rubs his head ecstatically on the scented pouch inside.

How to open the trap door and get to the treats?

Clever Bibi lifts the lid of the box with her head.

Even cats are willing to work for treats.

floor (see photos on page 64). Place the cloth over the wooden beads and let your cat play with it until he has uncovered the loot.

Roll up
Lay out a tea towel on the floor, place some treats on it and then screw up the tea towel. Your cat will watch you attentively, eagerly awaiting his chance to unpack the tasty prey. If you want to increase the skill level, place the food on the cloth, and then roll it up like a tortilla wrap.

This game requires no preparation and is easy to play, even after an exhausting day at work for cat owners.

Cats rely on their excellent sense of smell. If you want to give kitty a change, then not only hide a treat but also something slightly fragrant as well. A catnip mouse hidden under a towel will keep your cat busy for quite some time.

Please don't forget to deduct the food which is used as 'prey' from your cat's daily ration.

Kitten play area
Young cats have to play in order to improve physical and mental skills. Baby mats are not only ideal for small children, but also suitable for kittens. It only takes a few seconds to lay out the mat and then the journey of discovery can begin. The mats usually have a soft texture, and various little toys – such as buttons – sewn onto them. While one kitten investigates the toy frog, caterpillar, and ladybug, another is mesmerised by the glittering, mirror-like centre. And if the kittens get tired, they can simply lie down and take a nap.

Follow the trail!
For animals who are home alone during the day, it is particularly important to make the environment as exciting as possible. Hide treats all around the house, which your puss

On a child's play mat, kittens can observe, explore, hunt, and thus improve their physical and mental skills.

can track down. You can place the 'snacks' on shelves, in drawers, on chair seats, and so on. Make sure that your cat has access to these areas throughout the house, and, in the heat of the hunt, will not break anything.

After you return, those treats which have not been found will give you a clue to what your cat gets up to during the day!

Balancing act

If cats fall from a height of less than one metre, they could harm themselves, because there is

not enough time for a turning manoeuvre in the air. Of course, falling from a great height is worse, because the legs cannot withstand the force of the impact.

Water polo

For this game, you will need a wide container – for example, a bowl – and one soft and one hard rubber ball.

Fill the bowl with warm water and put the soft and hard ball in. You will see that your cat will first evaluate the situation and, after some time, he should come up with a solution to get the balls. Most cats will go for the soft rubber ball that floats on the water's surface, and use their paw to hook it out onto dry land. Water enthusiasts won't be afraid to dip their paw into the bowl to try and retrieve the ball which has sunk to the bottom.

A few animals may try an alternative approach, such as trying to drink the bowl empty in order to reach the toy!

If you use a transparent container, this makes it more difficult for the cat, as he can see the ball, but has to realise that he can only reach it from above.

Fetch!

Yes, you did read that right: many cats will play fetch when they feel like it. Some cats will quite naturally bring you a ball or a toy mouse and lay it at your feet. If you throw the toy, some cats will bring it back straightaway. Most cats, however, will have to be encouraged to do this.

Hold the toy in your hand, show it to your cat to make him curious. Then throw the mouse or the ball a couple of metres. If he fetches the toy, encourage and reward this behaviour with praise or treats. You can also offer him a different toy in exchange for the one he brings to you. Practice makes perfect, so repeat the exercise every day and your cat will learn that it pays to fetch the toy. Don't be disappointed if your cat shows no interest in doing this; not every cat likes this game.

Kit bits
FELINE BALANCE

Cats have an excellent sense of balance, and lightning-quick reactions to unexpected situations. The righting reflex – which uses the tail as a rudder – ensures that the cat rotates in free fall so that he lands on all four paws. A cat's inner ear has sensors that can perceive any motion in three dimensions, and therefore identify the orientation of the head, when in the air.

Fun and games for cats!

A Water-shy
Most cats are not that fond of water

B What's in there then?
Fishing a ball from a bowl of water is quite a challenge

C Hatching a plan
Willlow studies the bowl from all angles in order to figure out the appropriate hunting strategy

D Wet paws
She bravely dips her paw in and extends her claws to grip onto the rubber ball

E Gone fishing
With a well-aimed pat, the ball is retrieved from the water

Checklist: How clever is your cat?

	YES	NO
My cat shows that she wants to play with me using body language, or asks me by bringing her favourite toy	❏	❏
My cat often manipulates me to meet her demands	❏	❏
My cat asks when she wants a cuddle	❏	❏
My cat is confident and curious	❏	❏
My cat can interpret my moods and emotions	❏	❏
My cat is not stumped by brainteasers and locates the treat immediately	❏	❏
My cat can solve problems such as opening doors	❏	❏
My cat often watches me while I am busy in the house	❏	❏

Fun and games for cats!

If you answered 'yes:'

7-8 times
Congratulations! You have a super cat with a good brain who knows what she wants and how to get this idea across to you

3-6 times
Your cat is smart, and you can tap into her potential. Perhaps she is a cat who conserves her energy?

1-2 times
Your cat has not yet reached her potential. She may not feel challenged enough. Use some of the fun ideas in this book to inspire daily play-time and motivate your cat

Regular play sessions and attention strengthen the relationship between you.

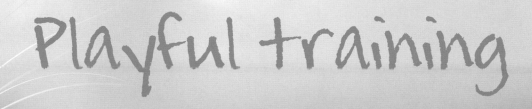

Playful training

Cats have minds of their own and usually do exactly as they please, although it is possible to train them to a certain extent. Through games we can get our domestic tigers to perform some tricks and correct any bad behaviour

Good kitty!

Is it possible to train a cat?

Living with a cat who has learned certain rules is easier and more harmonious. For example, there are situations where your cat should respond to his name; also, vet visits will be less stressful if she is accustomed to going into her carry box.

It's possible to make the lessons fun, as long as you are patient, and the training does not become stressful. On no account should you try and force your cat to do something.

The training will not be as automatic and effective as with a dog, because cats are fiercely independent creatures. Nevertheless, these four-legged hotshots are adaptable animals who are willing to respect certain accords, which means that compromise is possible if you provide the necessary incentive.

Training for owners
Respect and responsibility

Understand your cat with his unique characteristics and species-typical behavior.

Climbing, exploring, observing, hiding, hunting, and playing are basic behaviours that you should not deny your cat.

From a cat's perspective

Misunderstandings can be avoided if you are able to empathise with and understand your cat's behaviour.

Routine

Rituals, such as fixed feeding times, daily play and cuddle time make a cat feel secure, and strengthen the bond between the two of you.

Make sure you are consistent: if you choose to deny your cat something – maybe an item that he should not play with – then be consisent and stick to that. If you use the word 'no' to forbid something, always use this word. Constantly changing phrases, such as 'naughty cat!' or 'bad kitty!' etc, will confuse the animal and not achieve the desired result.

Timing

Whichever response you make to your cat, this must always immediately follow the action that precipitated it, as this is the only way the animal will be able to relate his behaviour to your reaction.

Correct or affirm his behaviour using praise or a treat, and a wrong deed with a loud 'no' within one to two seconds of the action. You will need to be really on the ball, because a couple of seconds longer than this and he won't make the connection.

Positive response

If a cat receives praise and encouragement, or attention from his owner, it's more likely that he will repeat the behaviour that elicited this.

No punishment

Punishing your cat will seriously damage the relationship between you, because the cat will henceforth be wary of what might happen, and withdraw from you. Punishment is never an option.

Realistic goals

When training, remember this rule: 'Small steps lead to success.' Don't try to get your cat to do any exercises that he can't perform because of age, fitness, etc.

Conditions

If you teach your cat a command or a trick, it should be in familiar surroundings and in a peaceful environment. One-to-one classes without anyone else watching guarantees

If the right incentives are offered, cats – despite their independent streak – are willing to compromise and accept certain rules.

your moggy's full attention. The practice sessions should only take place when your cat is fully alert, and never straight after he's eaten.

Communication

Good communication between humans and animals is a essential for successful training. Cats can judge your moods according to the sound, tone and volume of your voice, so when you talk to your cat, keep the tone calm and low, and the volume down. If you yell at your cat because the training isn't working, he will become scared and reluctant to participate in any further training.

Training basics

Every cat should have a name that is unique, and which suits his character and personality. He should run toward you, tail in the air, looking at you expectantly when called.

Cat names are usually one or two syllable words with the vowel sounds 'a' or 'e' and also 'o' or 'u'. Sharp sounds like 'sss' remind the animal of a hissing sound which may cause him to keep his distance. As is so often the case, it's the tone of your voice which says it all. Cats associate an action with a particular word. If you raise your tone in a lilting fashion when you say his name, when caressing, cuddling, playing and feeding him,

Most cats learn to respond to the sound of their name.

108

Being good for the sake of a treat, or some words of praise from his owner, is definitely worthwhile.

then he will make a positive association with the word. Your pet will come running over when you call him – provided he hasn't got anything better to do, that is!

Here!

You can try this when your cat is in a good mood, using a few tidbits as incentives.

Choose a verbal command which you will use again in future; maybe 'Here', or 'Come.' Hold a treat in your hand and call your cat by name. Take a step back, saying the command word you have chosen, and give him the treat when he reaches you. Gradually increase the distance between you and the animal so that, after a few exercises, your cat should come from a different room to you when you call, and appreciate the extra attention and treats he gets.

Only call your cat to you if he is nearby, or already on his way to you. If he is distracted by a noise or something else, wait until he gives you his full attention again. In order to make sure he participates, have treats at the ready which he can see. If he comes every time you call him, you'll know you've cracked it

Bibi waits expectantly for the start of her next exercise.

Even cats will sit on command ... if it suits them.

and won't need to give him a treat any more, though you should always praise him for doing as you ask.

'Sit' for cats

Hold a treat in your hand and run your hand over your cat's head toward his tail. Your cat will tilt his head to follow the treat's path and drop his hindquarters into a sitting position. As soon as he does this, give him the reward. As before, once he is reliably doing as you ask, exchange the treats for plenty of praise.

While many cats will come when called, 'sit' is one of the more difficult exercises. Be patient when the training does not go as smoothly as you'd like, and use the tasty treats as an incentive. When you say 'sit' point your finger at the same time. If your moggy is enjoying himself, he will soon learn to sit when he sees you do this, as long as he considers this fun and worthwhile.

Play therapy

Play is not only fun, it's also a remedy for boredom, invents adventures, keeps us physically and mentally fit, and improves social relationships.

Playing is synonymous with

communication, social contact, motivation, learning, education, and sport. It is, of course, pleasurable, and makes all animals feel happy.

Games can be played with abandon, alone, with other cats, or with you, his playmate. Regular play between two- and four-legged friends is the basis of a harmonious relationship, but if a cat is lacking in playful activities, he could demonstrate unpredictable behaviour in the home, and make a chaotic mess. A second cat is not always a guarantee that the animals will play with each other, and, in any case, even as a pair, they can become bored or frustrated. Often, they may simply be too different to socialise.

Influencing behavior

It is perfectly possible to influence any undesirable feline behaviour by playing with them. 'Play therapy' can change the basic rules of co-existence between man and animal, and also from cat to cat, and positive, social relationships will be formed. If cats have no way to live out their hunting instinct through playful activities, this can

lead to behavioural problems. An environment that addresses the natural needs of cats, and an activities or exercise programme will be a great help in avoiding this situation.

'Play therapy' should be individually created, according to character, activity level, health, age, and social environment. Every cat will have individual playing preferences.

With behavioural problems, 'play therapy' can achieve positive results, but it may also be a good idea to see an animal behavioural specialist if you are at all concerned about your cat's behaviour.

Attacks from behind

Young and adult cats alike love to launch layful attacks on their humans. Animals that

This mouse has extra-long, movable legs, and a long tail – great for a wild chase!

Fun and games for cats!

The owner's legs are often used as a climbing tree.

Just one of the many ways a cat tries to get attention from his people!

are alone during the day, or animals that are not kept busy enough, tend to show this kind of aggression. The cat lurks behind a piece of furniture, waiting for her chance to pounce on the legs of her owner when she walks by. The owner, taken by surprise, may exclaim, and possibly throw a toy to distract her cat, who is then rewarded for

Kit bits
LISTLESSNESS

The joy of playing should always be evident in your cat. If he no longer seems interested in playing, this could be an alarm signal. Find out whether the problem is physical or emotional, and investigate whether his living conditions could be the cause of his listlessness.

If cats are exhibiting problematic behaviour, there's usually always a reason for this. While we can respond to difficulties we encounter in many different ways, a cat uses bad behaviour to show his unhappiness and frustration.

this behaviour: just the kind of entertainment that your cat is looking for! Best to either voice a resounding 'No!' at the moment of attack and then ignore your cat for ten minutes, or attempt to redirect the attack to a toy, but be careful not to throw the toy too late or you will have rewarded your cat for his attack!

Night-time activities
Perhaps your cat is active during the night, running about the house, keeping you awake, and generally making a nuisance of himself.

Pouncing on your toes while you're lying in bed is a popular pastime which some owners try to fend off by distracting the cat with treats or attention. But Kitty quickly learns his attacks mean praise and yummy things, and whoever is feeding him the treats will most likely find their toes are pounced on even more. You have to ignore the nocturnal activities of your cat, so no treats, no petting, and no scolding! If his behaviour is ignored completely, he won't continue with it.

In the evening, make sure you play with him to use up excess energy so that you will both have a good night's sleep.

Destructive tendencies

In particular, young cats have a lot of energy and like to be on the go. If they can't find a suitable toy or a playmate with whom they can let off steam, their energy just builds and builds.

You're bound to have already experienced the usual feline 'mad five minutes' with your cat, when, suddenly and without warning, he will begin sprinting around and around the room, pouncing on anything in sight, and jumping on the sofa and shelves. After a few minutes of this frenetic activity, the storm is over and your puss is sitting peacefully on your lap. Other cats take this a step further and literally run up walls or curtains, and use their people as a climbing tree!

Relationship problems

Many cats are fearful of a particular family member, or another animal living in the same household, for example, a dog. Fun activities improve relationships between all species, so try and involve your dog in the fun! Don't be disappointed if your efforts are initially observed from a distance; it may take a while for each individual to decide that what you're doing looks like fun!

Trauma

Psychological stress caused by drastic changes in a cat's environment, or in the life of their humans, such as a divorce or a death in the family, can affect your cat, so be aware of this in these circumstances.

Weight

If a cat has no way of acting out hunting behaviour by playing games with you, he may attempt to offset boredom and stress by eating too much. Insufficient attention and an impaired human-animal relationship can both be underlying causes of obesity.

A bored cat with nothing to do could stir up trouble with his buddies.

Checklist: Are you the games-master?

1 Playing with my cat is
- ❑ a) a relaxed, pleasant pastime (0)
- ❑ b) the highlight of our relationship (5)
- ❑ c) an activity for the weekend (2)

2 I play with my cat
- ❑ a) after he's eaten (0)
- ❑ b) at dusk and into the evening hours (5)
- ❑ c) if he approaches me (2)

3 My puss is in the mood for boisterous play when
- ❑ a) he uses certain facial expressions and body language to show his playful mood (5)
- ❑ b) I encourage him with a treat (2)
- ❑ c) he has just settled in on the sofa (0)

4 If my cat suddenly decides he'd like to play
- ❑ a) I am usually too busy (0)
- ❑ b) I look for safe toys for him to play with (2)
- ❑ c) I make the most of the opportunity and get his favorite toys from the cupboard (5)

5 I play with my cat
- ❑ a) several times a day, for a total of one hour over the day (5)
- ❑ b) 2-3 times per week (2)
- ❑ c) rarely; I have several cats who play with each other (0)

6 A cat toy
- ❑ a) is a good substitute for daily play with my cat (0)
- ❑ b) I don't really need one. He has the freedom to roam where he wants (2)
- ❑ c) is a great way to provide fun for humans and animals (5)

7 I motivate my cat to play by

- ❏ a) rustling objects or making toys move in front of him (5)
- ❏ b) showing him his favorite toy (2)
- ❏ c) my cat is not interested in playing (0)

8 Play-time with my cat ends when

- ❏ a) one of us is tired (2)
- ❏ b) my cat has 'killed' the toy (5)
- ❏ c) he is defeated and cannot get the prey (0)

9 The cat activity tree is situated

- ❏ a) next to a window with a view (5)
- ❏ b) in the middle of the living room (2)
- ❏ c) in a quiet corner of the apartment to save on space (0)

10 What do you look for in the ideal toy for your cat?

- ❏ a) something which improves fitness and health and is lots of fun (5)
- ❏ b) we always play the same game (0)
- ❏ c) I buy the latest games (2)

Quiz results

31 points or over

Excellent result. You have really got the right idea and are definitely your cat's games-meister!

16–30 points

You are an advanced playmate and have got many things right. You have the right idea of collective hours of play with your cat, although maybe you and your cat could benefit from some inspiration

15 points and below

Play-time isn't really working for your cat, who may be bored, and probably pounces on you quite a lot. Remember that regular play is essential to prevent your cat getting bored and fed up, and becoming destructive or displaying other undesirable behaviour

Useful things

Further reading & websites

Further reading

Cat Speak: recognising and understanding behaviour by Brigitte Rauth-Widmann, Hubble & Hattie 2011, ISBN: 978-1845843854

Cats Handbook by David Alderton, Dorling Kindersley 2000, ISBN: 978-0751327762

What is my cat thinking? by Gwen Bailey, Hamlyn 2010, ISBN: 978-060061976

Indoor Cats by Katrin Behrend, Barron's Educational Series 2000, ISBN: 978-0764109355

Entertaining your indoor cat by Kevin Kelly, Sellers Publishing 2009, ISBN 978-1416205173

The Cat Whisperer by Claire Bessant, Blake Publishing 2004, ISBN: 978-1904034742 Kindle edition

Clicker training for Clever Cats by Martina Braun, Cadmos 2009, ISBN: 978-386127967

The Tiger on Your Couch by Bill Fleming & Judy Petersen-Fleming, Willian Morrow, 1994, ISBN: 978-0688135089

Playtime for Cats by Helena Dbaly & Stefanie Sigl, Cadmos 2009, ISBN: 978-3861279709

One Hundred Secret Thoughts Cats Have About Humans, by Celia Haddon, Hodder & Stoughton 2003, ISBN: 978-0340861707

Cat Counsellor: how your cat really relates to you by Vicky Halls, Bantam 2007, ISBN: 978-0553817621

Why Does My Cat ...? by Sarah Heath, Souvenir Press 2000, ISBN: 978-0285635494

Twisted Whiskers: Solving Your Cat's Behaviour Problems by Pam Johnson, Crossing Press 1994, ISBN: 978-0895947109

Understanding Cat Behaviour by Roger Tabor, David & Charles 2003, ISBN: 978-0715315897

The Cat Directory: Profiles of Every Cat Breed by David Taylor, Hamlyn 2010, ISBN: 978-0600620655

Miaow! Cats really are nicer than people! by Patrick Moore, Hubble and Hattie 2012, ISBN: 978-1845844356

Is Your Cat Crazy? Behaviour Problems and Solutions From the Casebook of a Cat Therapist by John C Wright, John Wiley & Sons 1996, ISBN: 978-0028608389

Websites

www.madcats.co.uk
The cat toy shop that has cat toys, cat accessories and cat supplies to pander to your feline's every need. Take a look – you won't be disappointed!

www.moggies.co.uk/plants
Lists houseplants that can be harmful or fatal to cats, depending on the quantity ingested

www.cattrees.co.uk
Quality cat trees, cat toys, and a large range of cat activity centres, with many unique designs in various colours to choose from

More great Hubble and Hattie books!

Cats really are nicer than people!

Sir Patrick Moore CBE FRS

Hubble & Hattie

£9.99*

cat
SPEAK

Hubble & Hattie

**recognising and
understanding
behaviour**

£9.99*

Animal Grief

HOW ANIMALS MOURN FOR EACH OTHER

Hubble&Hattie

DAVID ALDERTON

£9.99*

There seems little doubt that animals experience a range of emotions, just as we do; but can they grieve, too ...? This authoritative, rational text is superbly supported by interesting, sensitive photographs, carefully chosen to be reflective of the subject matter.

For more info about Hubble and Hattie books, visit www.hubbleandhattie.com • email info@ hubbleandhattie.com • Tel: 01305 260068 • *prices subject to change • p&p extra

The truth
ABOUT
wolves
& dogs

DISPELLING
THE MYTHS
OF DOG
TRAINING

Hubble & Hattie

TONI SHELBOURNE

£12.99*

A critique of traditional dog training and all the myths surrounding it, prompting the reader to look again at why we do certain things with our dogs. It corrects out-of-date theories on alpha status and dominance training, which have been so prominent over the years, and allows you to consider dog training afresh in order to re-evaluate your relationship with your canine companion, ultimately achieving a partnership based on mutual trust, love and respect.

Your dog will thank you for reading this book.

Index

Game notes

For Bitey Cat